W9-AET-804

Why'd They Do That?
Strange Customs of the Past

MUMMIFICATION

Gareth Stevens
Publishing

Alix Wood

Please visit our website, **www.garethstevens.com**. For a free color catalog of all our high-quality books, call toll free 1-800-542-2595 or fax 1-877-542-2596

Library of Congress Cataloging-in-Publication Data

Wood, Alix.
Mummification / by Alix Wood.
 p. cm. — (Why'd they do that? strange customs of the past)
Includes index.
ISBN 978-1-4339-9589-7 (pbk.)
ISBN 978-1-4339-9590-3 (6-pack)
ISBN 978-1-4339-9588-0 (library binding)
1. Mummies—Juvenile literature. 2. Civilization, Ancient--Miscellanea—Juvenile literature. I. Wood, Alix. II. Title.
GN293.W66 2014
393.3—dc23

First Edition

Published in 2014 by
Gareth Stevens Publishing
111 East 14th Street, Suite 349
New York, NY 10003

© Alix Wood Books

Produced for Gareth Stevens by Alix Wood Books
Designed and illustrated by Alix Wood
Picture and content research: Kevin Wood
Editor: Eloise Macgregor
Consultant: Rupert Matthews, the History Man

Photo credits: Cover, 1, 4, 5 left, 6, 7, 11 bottom right, 13 top right, 14 bottom, 15 bottom left, 16 bottom, 19, 21 top, 22, 28 top © Shutterstock; 3 and 29 bottom right © Patty Mooney; 8, 9 bottom, 14 right, 15 top, 15 bottom right, 16 inset, 18 © Trustees of the British Museum; 5 right © Jengod; 9 top © Einsamer Schütze; 13 bottom © Bullenwächter; 20 © Peter J. Bubenik; 23 top © Erik Meuser; 23 bottom © Mark Healey; 25 left © South Tyrol Museum of Archaeology – www.iceman.it; 25 bottom right © Jason Quinn; 26 © Cardenasg; 27 top © Pablo Trincado; 28 bottom © Michael Reeve; 29 top © Public Domain; 29 bottom left © Anatomist 90

Printed in the United States of America

CPSIA compliance information: Batch #CS13GS: For further information contact Gareth Stevens, New York, New York at 1-800-542-2595.

Contents

What is Mummification?

Mummification is the act of preserving a body. Mummies can be human or animal, and can be preserved either intentionally or accidentally. The bodies are preserved by exposure to chemicals, extreme cold, very low **humidity**, or lack of air. This exposure stops the body decaying.

The earliest ancient Egyptians buried their dead wrapped in goat hide in small pits in the desert. The heat and dryness of the sand **dehydrated** the bodies quickly, creating lifelike and natural mummies. The shifting sands of the desert made marking graves very difficult, so old graves would be accidentally disturbed when new graves were dug. The ancient Egyptians began burying their dead in coffins to protect them from this and from wild animals in the desert. The bodies placed in the coffins decayed, however.

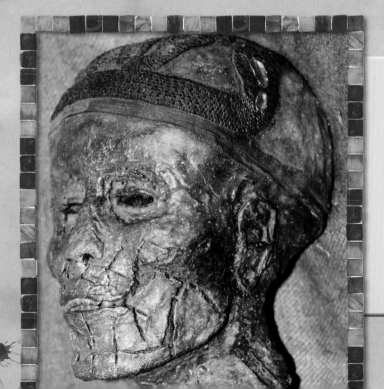

AFTERLIFE

Ancient Egyptians believed in an afterlife. Mummifying the body was important to preserve and protect it for the next life. This Egyptian mummy is amazingly well preserved.

Over many centuries, the ancient Egyptians developed a method of preserving bodies so they would remain lifelike. The process included embalming the bodies and wrapping them in strips of linen. Today we call this process mummification.

Mummies have been found all around the world. The oldest-known deliberate mummy is a child that was found in Chile, South America, and dates from around 5050 BCE.

REALLY?

Today, in San Bernardo, Colombia, close to 30 percent of bodies buried in the local cemetery become naturally mummified. Studies have been done but no one is sure what is causing the remains to mummify. It may be due to their diet rich in a local fruit, the chayote, or due to the climate or the altitude of the town. Mummies on display in the mausoleum are preserved almost completely with skin, hair, and even the clothes they were buried in!

A chayote

Osiris and Isis

The pharaoh Osiris was murdered by his jealous brother Set, who locked his body in a box and threw it into the River Nile. Isis, the pharaoh's wife, retrieved the box. Furious, Set chopped Osiris into many pieces and scattered them. Isis gathered up her husband's pieces and bandaged them back together in linen cloth.

With the help of Anubis, the god of the afterlife, and some powerful charms, Isis was able to bring Osiris back to life as a god. The myth of Osiris is the basis of why Egyptians believed mummification would ensure an afterlife. Osiris became the god of the afterlife. Anubis became the god of preservation of the bodies, and Isis was the protector of the dead.

The River Nile

A carving of Isis and Osiris from the temple of Osiris at Abydos, Egypt. Isis is wearing the horned crown of Hathor, the mother goddess.

REALLY?

A festival in honor of Osiris was held on the same day that the grain was planted. The festival involved the construction of seed beds in the shape of Osiris. The germinating seed in the beds symbolized Osiris rising from the dead.

THE EYE OF HORUS

In Egyptian mythology, after Osiris was brought back to life, he and Isis had a son called Horus. Horus wanted revenge for his father's murder. When Horus reached adulthood, he and Set fought a long battle. Horus won, but he lost his left eye in the fight. When Horus's eye was recovered, he offered it to his dead father. Horus's lost eye became a powerful symbol that enabled the dead to see again. The symbol of the eye of Horus became a necessary part of the mummification process. It was intended to protect the dead in the afterlife and to ward off evil. Horus was a sky **deity**; his right eye was said to be the sun and his left eye the moon.

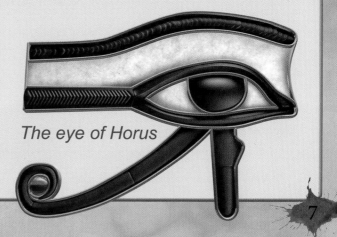

The eye of Horus

The Afterlife

The Egyptians thought that a person was made up of a body and two spirits, called the ba and the ka. When someone died, the body had to be complete, and the body and spirits had to be kept together. Ancient Egyptians believed that the ba spirit went out of the tomb every day and traveled through the **underworld**, and then came back to the body at night. If the ba could not recognize its body and return to it at night, then the ba would die. If the body was destroyed, the ka would die.

Even in the afterlife, there was work to do. Small models of servants, called shabtis, were placed in the tombs to help with the chores. The figures were made of wood, wax, metal, stone, or glazed ceramics. They were sometimes placed in model wooden coffins. The figures were often inscribed with text. Since most work was in the fields, many shabtis are shown carrying hoes, pickaxes, and baskets. At first only one shabti was placed in each tomb. Later tombs included large work gangs of shabtis with their own overseers.

Top, a shabti holding tools ready for work in the afterlife and bottom, a shabti in its coffin

THE GOD OF THE AFTERLIFE

Anubis oversaw the mummification of the dead for their journey into the afterlife. He is usually pictured as a jackal or a half-human, half-jackal. The jackal was associated with cemeteries in ancient Egypt, since it was a scavenger which was known to dig up human bodies and eat them. The black color symbolized the color of rotting flesh and the black soil of the Nile valley. In Egyptian mummification ceremonies, the **embalmer** would wear an Anubis costume.

eyeholes

An Anubis mask worn by the chief embalmers

Before the dead could enter the afterlife, they made a dangerous journey through the underworld. Special spells would help them on their way. The earliest texts of these spells were only available to royalty and were painted inside pyramids. As the texts became more available, they were painted on coffins. Later, the spells were recorded on a **papyrus** roll called the *Book of the Dead* and placed inside tombs.

REALLY?

On the journey through the underworld, the god Anubis would weigh the dead person's heart against an ostrich feather. If the heart was lighter than the feather, then the soul could pass on. If the heart was heavier, the soul would be eaten by Ammit, devourer of the dead.

Book of the Dead showing Anubis supervising the judgment scales watched by Ammit, part-crocodile, part-lion, and part-hippopotamus

Preserving the Body

Because a well-preserved body was necessary for life after death, the Egyptians went to great lengths to mummify the dead. The process took 70 days and was full of ritual. Embalmers used a salt called natron to remove moisture from the body and slow down **decomposition**.

First, the embalmers would take out the brain. A long hook was used to smash the brain up and then pull it out through the nose. Egyptians did not know the purpose of the brain, so they thought it was not worth keeping.

Then, a cut was made in the left side of the body to remove the internal organs. It was important to remove these because they were the first part of the body to decompose. The liver, lungs, stomach, and intestines were washed and packed in natron which dried them out. The heart was left in place because it was considered the center of intelligence and feeling.

CANOPIC JARS

Each of the person's organs was individually mummified, then stored in little coffins called canopic jars. There were four canopic jars, one for each of the organs. These jars were protected by the four sons of Horus, and each had one of their images on the top.

Qebehsenuef protected the intestines. He had the head of a falcon.

Ha'py watched over the lungs. He had the head of a baboon.

Duamutef looked after the stomach. He had the head of a jackal.

Imset protected the liver. He had the head of a human.

Next, the inside of the body was washed out with palm oil, lotions, and preserving fluids. The body was stuffed with packing material such as linen and straw to keep the general shape of the person. It was important not to overstuff or understuff the face or the mummy would look strange. To protect the mummy's face, a mask was placed over it. A pharaoh's mask would usually be made of gold. They sometimes put gold coverings over the fingers and toes to protect them.

REALLY?

Eyes were sometimes filled out with an onion or a stone!

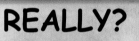

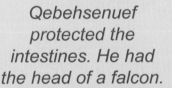

11

Wrapping the Mummy

Wrapping the body was a painstaking process. First a gold eye of Horus was placed over the slit in the abdomen to ward off evil. Hundreds of yards of linen were used to wrap the body. The wrapping process would be stopped in places so that the priests could say certain prayers, add charms, and write on the linen.

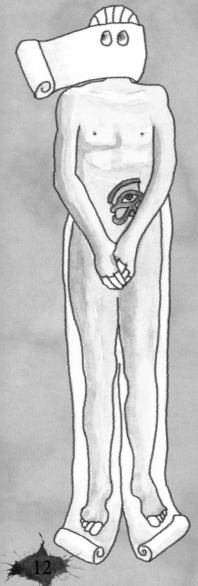

First the head and neck were wrapped with strips of fine linen. Then the fingers and the toes were individually wrapped. The arms and legs were wrapped separately.

A priest read spells out loud while the mummy was being wrapped. These spells were to help ward off evil spirits and help on the journey to the afterlife.

REALLY?

Charms, amulets, and papyrus texts were placed between each layer of bandage. Egyptians believed that these would protect the body.

This ancient Egyptian **hieroglyphic** *character meant "life."*

The ankh amulet above was often portrayed being held by Egyptian gods, one ankh in each hand, arms crossed over their chest.

The arms and legs were tied together. A papyrus scroll with spells from the *Book of the Dead* was placed between the wrapped hands.

At every layer, the bandages were painted with liquid resin to help glue them together.

This mummy's head has been very carefully wrapped.

A cloth was wrapped around the body, with a picture of the god Osiris painted on it. The mummy was wrapped in a large cloth and tied, with a board of painted wood placed on top. A painted portrait mask was placed over the mummy's head so that a dead person's ba could recognize its owner.

MUMMIA

A substance called mummia was added to the shroud to help glue it all together. This is where the word "mummy" comes from. Mummia also came to mean ground up mummies that were used in medicine and making paints.

Osiris's green skin symbolizes rebirth.

Into the Coffin

Once the body had been prepared and wrapped, a long ceremony called the opening of the mouth was performed to allow the deceased to eat, drink, breathe, and speak in the afterlife. A decorated coffin was made, painted with hieroglyphs praising the dead person. Wealthy people could have as many as three painted coffins placed inside each other.

Egyptian wooden coffins were beautifully crafted. Most of the wood had to be imported from other countries. The best wood was cedar from Lebanon. Carpenter's tools were not as efficient as the tools we have now, so the coffins must have taken a long time to make. The coffins would often be **gilded** with sheets of gold and painted with portraits of the dead, symbols, and heiroglyphs. The nest of coffins would then be placed in a large stone coffin called a sarcophagus once at the tomb.

Black siltstone sarcophagus

Wooden painted coffin

14

REALLY?

The opening of the mouth ceremony used a calf's leg cut from a live calf! This picture is of the ceremony at the scribe Hunefer's funeral in his *Book of the Dead.*

calf's leg used in ceremony

Hunefer's mummy

Anubis

tools for the ceremony

three-legged calf

Modern copy of Tutankhamun's gold funerary mask

THE FUNERAL

At the funeral **mourners** would wear blue. Sometimes mourners would be hired to attend and would not even know the deceased. The weighing of the heart ceremony would take place, and then the coffin and all the grave goods would be carried or pulled on a sledge to the tomb. Grave goods would often include a headrest, a chest, a wig box, a game, wine, food, and shabtis.

Meryrahashetef's headrest shaped to resemble two hands

Pyramids

The pyramids are the stone tombs of Egypt's pharoahs. The biggest pyramid is the Great Pyramid at Giza. It took more than 2 million blocks of stone to build, each weighing around 1.5 tons. The ancient Egyptians had to use ropes and sledges to move the blocks. They piled up vast ramps of soil to get the blocks to the top. Their tools were simple, made of wood, stone, or copper. Tens of thousands of people worked to build the pyramids.

The Great Pyramid took 23 years to finish. It is believed to have been built for the pharaoh Khufu. The mummies and treasure that were placed in the tombs were stolen long ago. The grave goods were very tempting for grave robbers, who would know there would be great riches inside the pyramids.

REALLY?

Often cats and other animals would be mummified and put into the tombs. Cats were **revered** by Egyptians.

The Great Pyramid

On the seventieth day after a person's death, the coffin was taken to the tomb. Two women dressed as Isis and her sister Nephthys walked behind the coffin. The mourners, priests, and servants carrying tomb furnishings followed. The canopic chest with its jars of organs was carried separately. Priests burned **incense** and sprinkled milk along the path. At the tomb, the group was met by dancers and a priest who read texts in honor of the dead. The mourners ate a banquet while the coffin was placed inside the tomb. The footprints of those who had been inside were swept away, and the door was shut and sealed. Let's hope none of the mourners got left behind by accident.

A mummy on its sledge, followed by the funeral procession

INSIDE THE GREAT PYRAMID

The mummy was kept deep inside the pyramid. It must have been very difficult for the coffin bearers to drag the coffin up the slopes and into the tomb. The ceilings were low and the coffin would be very heavy. There was no natural light, no heat, and only muffled sound deep inside the pyramid. The underground chamber seems to be unfinished. No one is too sure what the shaft from the gallery to the underground chamber was used for.

King's chamber

Grand gallery

Queen's chamber

Shaft

Pit

Underground chamber

Care in the Tomb

The burial of the pharaoh was not the end to the process! Every day, the chief priest and his followers would go to the chapel next to the pyramid. Inside stood a statue of the dead pharaoh, and behind it was a false door, which the ba was thought to fly in and out of. The priests would wash the statue and cover it with perfumed oils. The priests also left food and wine in front of the false door at regular intervals.

Egyptians believed that if people remembered you and spoke your name you would enjoy everlasting life. In his lifetime, a pharaoh acted as intermediary between Egypt's people and the gods. When a pharaoh died, he became a god. Many temples were dedicated to the worship of deceased pharaohs. Over time, families would gradually forget to take offerings to long-dead relatives. Most dead pharoahs were only remembered for one or two generations. However, the living sometimes wrote letters asking deceased relatives for help, in the belief that the dead could affect the world of the living as the gods did.

A false door. The door has pictures of the pharoah, his wife, and his son and daughter. It would once have been brightly painted.

A booby-trapped corridor

To protect the mummy after its burial, pyramid builders constructed secret passages, dead-ends, and booby traps to fool any tomb robbers. Secret doors to burial chambers would sometimes be hidden behind a statue. They would build **decoy** rooms with a few items of treasure, while the actual burial chamber was somewhere else. Secret passages were used to trick robbers into entering booby-trapped rooms. Rocks would be balanced on the tops of doors and deep holes were covered with flimsy lids that collapsed under a man's weight. Wires were strung across at neck height to cut off a fleeing robber's head.

REALLY?

Often, grave goods were also painted or carved on the tomb walls. The Egyptians believed that pictures, models, or written words could magically become real themselves if the original items were destroyed or lost.

KA FOOD

It was believed that food left by the false door of the tomb would be consumed by the ka of the deceased. The priests would return later and clear any uneaten food away. They probably got some good meals!

Figs, grapes, and bread were popular offerings.

Digging Up Mummies

The great days of ancient Egypt ended and slowly people forgot how to mummify a body or to read hieroglyphs. Robbers looted every tomb they could find. It wasn't just the treasure that the robbers were after. Mummies became very fashionable!

People began to want to understand the secrets of the Egyptian tombs. Code-breakers worked out how to read hieroglyphs. **Archaeologists** tried to find a tomb which had not been robbed. In 1922 that dream came true. An Englishman, Howard Carter, found a hidden door in the Valley of the Kings. He broke through and found the mummified body of the pharaoh Tutankhamun. The surrounding rooms were filled with treasures which had not been disturbed for thousands of years. The pharaohs had realized that a pyramid was too obvious a place to hide a tomb, and chose a valley instead.

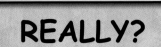

LORD LONDESBOROUGH
At Home,
MONDAY, 10th JUNE, 1850
144 PICCADILLY

A Mummy from Thebes to be unrolled at half-past Two.

To _____ No._____

REALLY?

Mummy unwrappings were popular. This invite wasn't really a party, though. Most of the people who went were members of a history society.

The remote Valley of the Kings, where Tutankhamun's tomb was discovered

Tutankhamun was buried in a tomb that was small considering his status. As he died aged 19, his death may have occurred unexpectedly before the completion of a grander royal tomb. His mummy was probably buried in a tomb intended for someone else. The discoveries in the tomb were international news in the 1920s.

A replica of the golden throne found in Tutankhamun's tomb. The pharaoh and queen Ankhesenamun are pictured on the back rest.

101 USES FOR A DEAD MUMMY

In the 12th century, Arab physicians began to prescribe their patients a very unusual medicine, the ground remains of mummies! The mummy powder was sold in a variety of strengths. Powder made from peasants buried in sand pits only relieved minor stomachaches. The mummified Egyptian aristocracy were capable of healing life-threatening wounds. Egyptian tombs were ransacked for bodies to be made into medicine. Unscrupulous salesmen began to dry out the bodies of executed criminals and the unburied poor to turn into mummy powder.

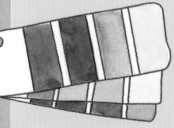

In the 16th and 17th centuries, ground mummy was also the key ingredient in a popular shade of brown artist's pigment, called "mummy brown" until the early 20th century.

American author Mark Twain claimed that mummies with a high content of petroleum-based **bitumen** were also used as coal to power the engines of the locomotives on the new railroads in North Africa.

Natural Mummies

Mummification can happen naturally in the right environments. Cold peat bogs, dry deserts, and freezing temperatures can all help to preserve a body. This exposure stops the body decaying. While many mummifications happen accidentally in these environments, some cultures would use the conditions to preserve their loved ones intentionally.

Peat formed from rotted moss and other plants creates airless and acidic conditions, perfect for preserving dead bodies. During the Iron Age (1200 BCE–400 CE), peat bogs covered a large area of northern Europe. Many bodies have been found preserved in the peat bogs. Experts believe the bogs held some sort of importance to the people living near them at that time. They placed offerings into them for the gods. It is believed that the bog bodies were placed in the bog for similar reasons, as offerings in the form of human **sacrifice** to the gods.

Peat can be used as a fuel when it dries. Bodies have been unearthed by people digging for the fuel.

MUMMY MURDER

In 1950 some villagers were digging up peat in a bog near Tollund, Denmark. Suddenly, they saw a human face staring up at them. Investigations into the mummy showed that it had been there for at least 2,000 years. The man had been murdered. Tied round his neck was a length of rope, which had also been preserved in the peat along with the man's sheepskin cap and leather belt. He had been strangled or hanged and laid carefully in the bog. It is believed this was a ritual killing, as other similar bodies have been found in the same area.

The Tollund Man is hardly decayed at all. His fingers and toes have been perfectly preserved, and you can even see the stubble on his chin! The rope used to strangle him is still around his neck.

REALLY?

A bog body's skin is turned dark by the acidity of the water, cold temperature, and lack of oxygen which tans the skin and soft tissues.

Clonycavan Man (below) was found in Ireland in March 2003. He is remarkable for his Mohawk hairstyle and his hair gel of plant oil and pine resin! His skull had been split open, probably by an axe.

Frozen Mummies

Frozen mummies have been found in many of the coldest places in the world. Some of the best-preserved natural mummies date from the Inca period in Peru and Chile around 500 years ago, where children were ritually sacrificed on the summits of mountains in the Andes.

In 1995 two archaeologists climbed a mountain in Peru in South America to photograph a smoking volcano nearby. Near the top, they spotted a bright red feather headdress in the ice. Just below it, they found a bundle wrapped in sacking, with the dried-out face of a girl staring out at them. The child has become known as the Ice Maiden. She had been buried alive on the mountaintop as a sacrifice to please the gods about 500 years ago. The freezing temperatures had preserved her body. Unlike the Egyptian mummies, her body was complete, with the heart and other organs still in place.

The Ice Maiden is also sometimes called Mummy Juanita.

ÖTZI THE ICEMAN

Ötzi was found by two tourists walking in the Ötztal Alps on the border between Austria and Italy. He is Europe's oldest natural human mummy, from around 3300 BCE. At first people believed that Ötzi died from exposure during a winter storm. It now appears that he was the victim of a ritual sacrifice. He had an arrowhead lodged in his left shoulder and a matching small tear on his coat. He also had other wounds.

Some people think Ötzi is cursed. Seven mysterious deaths have happened to people connected with Ötzi's discovery. Hundreds of other people involved in the recovery are fine though!

A reconstruction of what Ötzi would have looked like

REALLY?

In the Tarim Basin in China, several mummies have been found, preserved with complete bodies and organs. They are able to be moved and have their joints bent with care. Oddly, these mummies were Europeans.

This is a model of an Incan child mummy found on Cerro El Plomo in Chile in 1954. It was the first frozen Inca sacrifice mummy discovered on a mountain.

Dry Climate Mummies

Deserts can be very hot—and very cold. Mummies found in the deserts of South America had been preserved by both the baking dry heat and the chilling winds. In the hot, dry Canary Islands, off the coast of Spain, corpses were preserved by simply being wrapped up in goat and sheep skins.

The people of the Canary Islands also embalmed their dead. Their method was similar to that of the ancient Egyptians. In Tenerife, the corpse was wrapped in animal skins, while on other islands, a **resinous** substance was used to preserve the body, which was then placed in a cave or buried under a mound. The work of embalming was done by women for female corpses and by men for males.

REALLY?

Some Buddhist monks used to practice self-mummification. If the monk was successful, their mummy was seen as a Buddha and put in the temple for viewing. One monk who died around 1475 starved himself before his death and gradually suffocated using a belt tied around his neck and his knees while sitting cross-legged. His body was found, well preserved, in the 1970s. Some monks were buried alive in a wooden box full of salt!

This mummy from Tenerife is kept in special dry conditions so it does not decompose.

CHINCHORRO MUMMIES

The Chinchorro mummies from the Pacific coast of Chile and southern Peru are the oldest deliberately prepared mummified bodies ever found, ranging from about 5000–3000 BCE. The bodies were mummified using different techniques at different periods. The cold, dry climate also helped preserve them. While many cultures mainly only preserved important people, the Chinchorro mummified all members of their society.

A Chinchorro mummy. The black color is a result of black manganese which was painted on the skin.

The mummies were prepared in a variety of ways. One method involved the dead person's head, arms, and legs being removed, treated, and reassembled. The skin was often removed, too. The body was then heat-dried. After reassembly, the body was then covered with a white ash paste, filling the gaps with grass, ashes, soil, and animal hair. The paste was also used to recreate the person's face. The skin was put back on the body, sometimes in smaller pieces, sometimes in one large piece. Sea lion skin could be used as well. The skin was painted with black **manganese**, which gives the mummies their color.

Mummies Now

Some people believe that a technique for freezing bodies, called cryopreservation, may mean that their bodies can be preserved until a cure for whatever they died of has been found. Modern body preservation methods are cryopreservation, plastination, and embalming. The reasons why people get their bodies preserved may have changed, but the practice still occurs even today.

Jeremy Bentham was a British philosopher and social reformer who wished to have his body preserved after his death in 1832. The skeleton and head were preserved and stored in a wooden cabinet, with the skeleton padded out with hay and dressed in Bentham's clothes. He was acquired by University College, London, in 1850. He is normally kept on public display in the main building of the college, but for the 100th and 150th anniversaries of the college he was brought to the College council meeting, where he was listed as "present but not voting"!

His head looked a little macabre, with dried, darkened skin stretched over the skull. He was given a new wax head, fitted with some of Bentham's own hair. The real head was also displayed in the same case for many years, but became the target of student pranks and is now locked away securely!

Jeremy Bentham in his cabinet

Elmer McCurdy was a bank and train robber who was killed in a gunfight. His last words were "You'll never take me alive!" His body was taken to a funeral home. When no one claimed the corpse, the undertaker embalmed it and charged people to see "The Bandit Who Wouldn't Give Up." People would place nickels in McCurdy's mouth as payment. For the next 60 years, McCurdy's body was sold to wax museums, carnivals, and haunted houses. During filming of the television show *The Six Million Dollar Man* (1977) at an amusement park in Long Beach, California, a crew member was moving what he thought was a wax mannequin hanging from a gallows. When its arm broke off, it was discovered that the model was the mummified McCurdy! A 1924 penny and a ticket from Sonney Amusement's Museum of Crime in Los Angeles were found in his mouth!

WANTED

ELMER MCCURDY

DEAD OR ALIVE

PLASTINATION

Plastination is a technique used to preserve bodies or body parts. Water and fat are replaced by plastics. After soaking in a chemical solution and put in a frozen vacuum, other chemicals draw out all the water. In a bath of liquid polymer, such as

A plastinated arm

silicone rubber, the cells are filled with liquid plastic. The plastic must then be cured with gas, heat, or ultraviolet light in order to harden it. In the early 1990s, it became possible to plastinate a whole body. The inventor, Gunther von Hagens, held public exhibitions, showing whole bodies plastinated in lifelike poses and cut open to show various structures and systems of the human **anatomy**.

A plastinated face

Glossary

anatomy
A branch of knowledge that deals with the structure of organisms.

archaeologists
Scientists that deal with past human life as shown by fossil relics and the monuments and tools left by ancient peoples.

bitumen
A sticky, black, tar-like substance.

decomposition
Breaking down, rotting away.

decoy
Something intended to lure into a trap.

dehydrated
Having lost water or bodily fluids.

deity
A god.

embalmer
Someone who treats a dead body with special preparations to preserve it from decay.

gilded
Covered with or as if with a coating of gold.

hieroglyphic
Describing a pictorial system of writing, such as ancient Egyptian.

humidity
The amount of moisture in the air.

incense
A material used to produce a fragrant odor when burned.

manganese
A grayish white, usually hard and brittle metallic element that resembles iron but is not magnetic.

mourners
People grieving over someone's death.

papyrus
Strips of a tall grass pressed into a kind of paper and then written on.

resinous
With the properties of resin, a substance obtained from the gum or sap of some trees.

revered
Showed devotion and honor to.

sacrifice
An act of offering something precious to God or a god.

underworld
The place of the souls of the dead.

For More Information
Books

Hynson, Colin. *You Wouldn't Want to Be an Inca Mummy! A One-Way Journey You'd Rather Not Make.* Franklin Watts, 2007.

Putnam, James. *Mummy.* DK Publishing, 2009.

Sloan, Christopher. *Mummies: Dried, Tanned, Sealed, Drained, Frozen, Embalmed, Stuffed, Wrapped, and Smoked...and We're Dead Serious.* National Geographic Children's Books, 2010.

Websites

Mummy Maker
kids.discovery.com/games/just-for-fun/mummy-maker
Play this fun educational game to test if you know how to make a mummy.

Mummy Tombs
www.mummytombs.com
This website is full of information on all types of mummies. It has details of museums to visit and projects to try.

Publisher's note to educators and parents: Our editors have carefully reviewed these websites to ensure that they are suitable for students. Many websites change frequently, however, and we cannot guarantee that a site's future contents will continue to meet our high standards of quality and educational value. Be advised that students should be closely supervised whenever they access the Internet.

Index